IF YOU SAILED
On the
Titanic

TITANIC

With special thanks to Philip Hind.

Text copyright © 2023 by Denise Lewis Patrick
Illustrations copyright © 2023 by Winona Nelson

Library of Congress Cataloging-in-Publication Data Available

ISBN 978-1-338-77719-2 (paperback) / 978-1-338-77720-8 (hardcover)

10 9 8 7 6 5 4 3 2 1   23 24 25 26 27

Printed in China   38
First edition, January 2023

Book design by
Jaime Lucero and Brian LaRossa

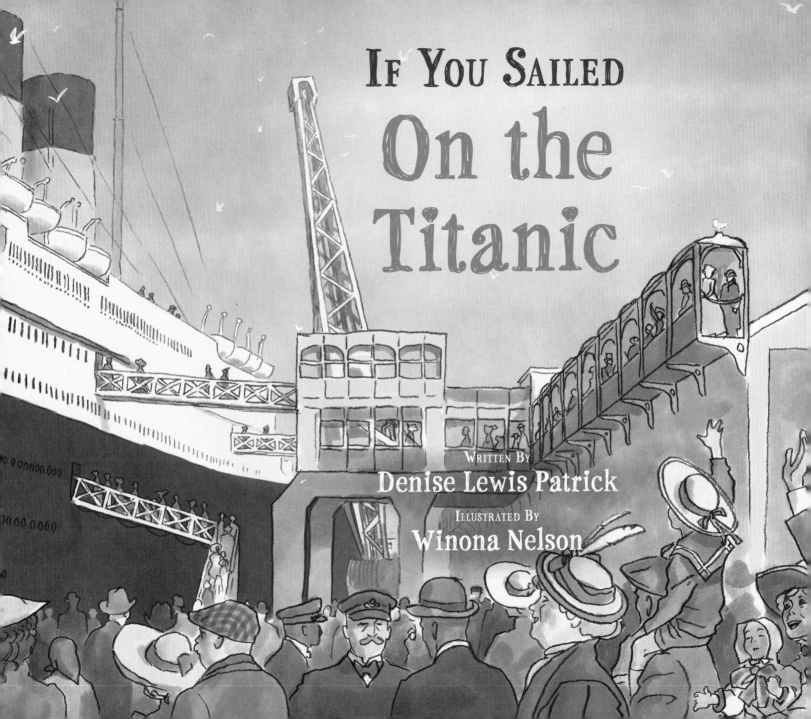

IF YOU SAILED
On the
Titanic

WRITTEN BY
Denise Lewis Patrick

ILLUSTRATED BY
Winona Nelson

Table of Contents

Introduction

If you had set sail on the *Titanic*, you would have been looking forward to an amazing experience on the largest ocean liner ever built. You may have been a wealthy traveler who was used to grand hotels and excellent meals. You might have been a young sailor, excited about crossing the Atlantic Ocean for the first time. Or, you and your family might have been leaving the life you knew behind, hoping to find a wonderful new home in America.

Whatever your dreams might have been, everything would have changed in the middle of one dark night when the unexpected happened to the "unsinkable" *Titanic*.

What was the *Titanic*?

The *Titanic* was a **transatlantic** ocean liner that set out on its maiden, or first, voyage across the Atlantic Ocean on April 10, 1912. At that time, airplane travel was not common or affordable. Travelers relied on trains to cross long distances on land, and on ships to make ocean crossings.

At the time, the *Titanic* was already world-famous. Although other ships were more glamorous, none were the *Titanic*'s size. Newspapers around the world reported on every detail about the ship as it was constructed and completed, especially its modern additions like elevators and a heated pool.

Most people believed the *Titanic* was unsinkable.

Why was the *Titanic* built?

Competition was fierce among transatlantic shipping companies at the turn of the twentieth century. More and more people wanted to make the crossing from the United States to Europe and back again. There were successful French and German shipping companies working in the North Atlantic Ocean. Perhaps two of the biggest rivals were both British companies—the White Star Line and the Cunard Line.

In 1904, J. Bruce Ismay was both chairman and managing director of the White Star Line. He was the son of the company's founder. Ismay wanted to show the shipping world that he could keep running the company successfully after his father died in 1899. He had to find a way to outdo Cunard.

J. BRUCE ISMAY

Cunard was well-known for the **luxury** of its ocean liners. They were one of the first to add electric lights and wireless communication to their ships. And Cunard's ships had broken speed records, winning shipping's "Blue Riband" honor for the fastest Atlantic crossing. But Ismay decided to forget about speed, and set out to beat Cunard with size, comfort, and luxury.

He teamed up with the White Star Line's shipbuilder, Harland and Wolff. After conversations with his friend Lord William Pirrie (part owner of Harland and Wolff), Ismay had a plan.

His vision was to create three "Olympic-class" ships. Harland and Wolff would build them, of course, and use the latest construction methods for the ships' **hulls** and engines. They would all have both electric lights and heat—even heated swimming pools! Their telegraph room would be designed by the Marconi company, owned by the inventor of wireless communication himself, Guglielmo Marconi.

They might not be faster than Cunard's ships, but because

they could carry more passengers and more cargo than any others in the world, the new ships would make more money for the White Star Line.

Ismay decided to call them, in order of their completion: *Olympic*, *Titanic*, and *Britannic*.

How did the *Titanic* get its name?

The name *Titanic*, and that of its "sister" ship, *Olympic*, came from Greek mythology. According to legend, the Titans were a race of giant, all-powerful beings who ruled the world and could live forever. The word "titan" has come to mean gigantic, or powerful. That's exactly how Ismay wanted the world to think of his new ships.

The *Titanic*'s official name was actually RMS *Titanic*. The RMS stood for Royal Mail Steamer (later, Royal Mail Ship), because the *Titanic* was under contract to transport mail across the Atlantic.

How long did it take to build the *Titanic?*

Bringing Ismay and Pirrie's "Olympic" idea to life didn't happen overnight. First, they brought their plan to Harland and Wolff's shipyard in Belfast, Ireland.

It took a full year just to draw up designs for the first two ships, *Olympic* and *Titanic.* Their construction would happen at the same time. One of the first problems Harland and Wolff faced was that the new ships would be so big that the Belfast shipyard had to be enlarged to make room for them. In New York, the White Star Line's pier, where the ships would dock, also had to be made longer.

Work on *Olympic* began first, in December 1908. In March 1909, the **keel** was laid for the *Titanic.* With this long, bladelike "backbone" of the ship in place, construction of the hull began. Nearly three million iron and steel rivets, or bolts, held the steel hull together. Riveting crews worked six days a week, with half days on Saturdays. The *Titanic's* massive hull was completed in May 1911, more than two

years after construction started. It launched from the shipyard into the deep water of the Victoria Channel.

Next came the "fitting-out" of the rest of the ship. Workers built smokestacks and installed engines, furnaces, and water tanks. They built kitchens and staircases and walls. They carved woodwork and ran electrical wires.

One of Harland and Wolff's newest safety features was installed on the *Titanic*: sixteen water-tight compartments

below deck. In case of a flooding emergency, the compartments could be sealed off by flipping a switch. Because of this system, the ship could stay afloat even if three of the compartments were completely flooded. Of course, no one at the time knew how important this feature would be.

However, even with all the hard work, the *Titanic*'s sea trials and maiden voyage were delayed twice so that *Olympic* could be completed on time.

Finally, three years after the keel was laid, the *Titanic* was finished and ready to sail at the end of March 1912.

When it was completed, the ship was 882 feet long (more than twice the length of a US football field) and 92 feet wide. There were ten decks. It was over 170 feet tall from the keel to the top of its smokestacks—taller than the Statue of Liberty from her heel to the top of her head. The *Titanic*'s top speed was 21–23 knots, or about 24–27 miles per hour.

It took the skills of about 3,000 of Harland and Wolff's 15,000 employees to turn Ismay and Pirrie's dream ships into reality.

Although *Olympic* and *Titanic* were just alike in many ways, the builders made changes to the *Titanic*'s interior to create more space for passenger cabins and restaurants. These improvements edged the *Titanic* past her sister ship to become the largest ocean liner in the world.

How much did the *Titanic* cost to build?

Back in 1902, five years before the *Titanic* was even thought of, the White Star Line **merged** with a shipping company owned by American banker J. P. Morgan.

Many British businessmen and citizens weren't happy with this American "takeover" of such an important British company. But Morgan allowed the White Star Line to remain under British control, and his money made it possible for the White Star Line to grow.

The company spent a whopping $7,500,000 to build the *Titanic*. That amount is close to two hundred million dollars today!

Who was the captain of the *Titanic*?

By the time Edward J. Smith became captain of the RMS *Titanic*, he had worked at sea for more than half his life.

EDWARD J. SMITH

Smith was born in England in 1850. When he was a teenager, he left school to join the merchant navy. He worked his way up from crewman to more important jobs on cargo ships transporting goods between England and South America.

Smith made the move to ocean liners (ships that carry paying passengers) when he was hired by the White Star Line in 1880. His first command of a passenger ship was a few years later, on the White Star Line's *Baltic*. From 1895 to 1904, Captain Smith also served as a reserve officer in the British Royal Navy.

Over his years with the White Star Line, Smith was given charge of larger and more expensive ships. Due to his experience, he was granted command of the *Olympic* when she was completed in 1911. The *Olympic* sailed between New York and England for nearly a year before it was damaged in an accident with a British navy ship and taken out of service for repairs.

Smith was selected for his next, and final, command aboard the *Titanic* in 1912.

In the days after the *Titanic* disaster, many people questioned the captain's actions and decisions on the night the ship sank. Even though Smith received telegraphs, or wireless messages, earlier in the day warning that icebergs had been spotted in the area, he apparently never gave an order to reduce the speed of the ship in order to navigate the area more safely. In addition, when he ordered the *Titanic's* lifeboats to be lowered, he allowed some of them to leave before they were completely full. This left many second- and third-class passengers with no way to escape the sinking ship.

Some surviving crew members and passengers considered Smith a hero. However, both the US and the

British investigations of the disaster found that Smith was partially responsible for what happened.

No one disputed the fact that Smith had followed two traditional rules of the sea. First, he insisted that the women and children evacuate before the men. Second, and most important, he remained on board after all the lifeboats had left. The captain went down with his ship.

Where did the *Titanic* sail from?

When the construction of the *Titanic* was completed, the ship sailed from Belfast to Southampton, where its voyage officially began. The planned route was from Southampton to Cherbourg, France, to Queenstown (now known as Cobh), Ireland, and then on to New York City.

In Southampton, the *Titanic*'s crew and captain boarded, as well as passengers from London, England, and other parts of the United Kingdom who arrived by train. At noon on April 10, 1912, the ship headed for Cherbourg to take on more passengers. It left France that same evening.

The *Titanic*'s final European stop was at Queenstown port on the morning of April 11. Many of the passengers who boarded there were hoping to **immigrate** to America. The ship also took on bags of mail for delivery in the United States.

That afternoon, the *Titanic* raised its anchor and set sail on the longest leg of its journey.

How were passengers grouped?

Passengers were organized into three groups: first class, second class, and third class. The main difference between these groups was how the people in them ranked in the society of 1912.

Nearly all the first-class passengers were American or British. These were extremely wealthy or very important people—and in many cases, they were both. Among the Americans were millionaires John Jacob Astor IV and Benjamin Guggenheim, as well as Isidor Straus, owner of Macy's Department Store, and his wife, Ida. Also on board was the White Star Line's owner J. Bruce Ismay. Other first-class passengers included an aide to then–US president William Howard Taft and a famous British fashion designer.

One first-class passenger described the *Titanic* as "a floating palace," and it was true that the first-class experience was like staying at a fancy hotel. Almost all of their activities were separate from those of the second- or third-class passengers and were located on the upper decks of the ship. There were several different first-class dining rooms and cafés. There was a library, a full gym, and a huge **promenade** for outdoor walking. Their sleeping quarters were beautifully decorated. The largest of these were suites, each of which was the size of a small apartment. The suites included a bedroom, bathroom, living room (with a fireplace), and even a private promenade.

Second-class passengers included a mix of different people. Some were tourists and families who had spent their vacation traveling around England and other European countries. Some were teachers or businessmen. A few were nannies or servants of the first-class passengers. Second-class rooms were shared cabins with either two or four bunk beds. These passengers shared bathrooms.

Third-class cabins—also called steerage—were down on the lowest decks of the ship, tucked around the loud engines. Up to ten people slept in one cabin. Families stayed together, but single men and women had separate spaces.

The 709 third-class passengers only had two bathrooms to share among themselves! But for many of them this was still a luxury, since they didn't have indoor plumbing at home.

The lives of the *Titanic*'s passengers were separated aboard the ship in the same way they were on land because of their different levels of education, wealth, and experiences. They rarely, if ever, mixed with one another.

How much did a ticket cost?

The prices of tickets for the full crossing (from England to America) were set based on passenger class. Here are the average prices in US dollars in 1912, and the estimated cost today:

	1912	2021
First class	$150 (cabin) $4,350 (suite)	$4,300 (cabin) $124,650 (suite)
Second class	$60	$1,720
Third class	$15–$40	$430–$1,146

Where did the passengers come from?

In many ways, the *Titanic* was a world of its own, carrying passengers from at least forty-four different countries. They came from some of the largest cities in the world, as well as from small towns and tiny villages.

Citizens of countries on every continent except Antarctica were aboard the *Titanic*. There were people from India, China, Japan, and Thailand; from Russia and Bulgaria; from Cuba, Haiti, and Mexico; from Egypt and South Africa. Europeans on board came from places such as France, Germany, the Netherlands, Belgium, and Spain.

Apart from the Americans and the British, the largest groups of travelers were from Ireland, Sweden, and what is now Lebanon. Most of them were third-class passengers seeking to immigrate to America.

Altogether, the *Titanic* carried an estimated 2,208 passengers and crew.

What was daily life like for passengers on the *Titanic*?

The White Star Line offered its passengers a great variety of ways to enjoy their six-day voyage.

A first-class passenger could take the grand staircase with its glass-domed ceiling to eat breakfast in one of the

dining rooms. Afterward, they might take a stroll outside on the grand promenade. Or, they could choose to relax in the reading room with a book from the ship's first-class library.

Boys and girls might play with their toys or run along the promenade, then play a game of chess or shuffleboard. They could check out the heated pool—something only the *Titanic*'s sister ship *Olympic* had. There was a squash court, barbershop, and steam room. In the evenings, the orchestra played music and took song requests from passengers.

However, between first-, second-, and third-class passengers, the choices for entertainment were somewhat different.

The musicians sometimes played in second class, too. Second-class passengers also had their own library and reading room, a large dining room, and an outdoor promenade.

In third class, there was a promenade and a large room for socializing. This gathering space had a piano so that passengers could make their own music for entertainment. And unlike steerage passengers on many other ships, those on the *Titanic* didn't have to bring their own food—they had their own dining room.

All passengers were served three meals a day, but a look at one day's breakfast menus for each group shows that those meals were not quite the same.

WHITE STAR LINE

April 14, 1912

1ST CLASS

BREAKFAST

BAKED APPLES   FRESH FRUIT   STEWED PRUNES
QUAKER OATS   BOILED HOMINY   PUFFED RICE
FRESH HERRINGS

FINNAN HADDOCK   SMOKED SALMON
GRILLED MUTTON   KIDNEYS & BACON
GRILLED HAM   GRILLED SAUSAGE
LAMB COLLOPS   VEGETABLE STEW
FRIED, SHIRRED, POACHED & BOILED EGGS
PLAIN & TOMATO OMELETTES TO ORDER
SIRLOIN STEAK & MUTTON CHOPS TO ORDER
MASHED, SAUTÉ & JACKET POTATOES
COLD MEAT
VIENNA & GRAHAM ROLLS
SODA & SULTANA SCONES   CORN BREAD
BUCKWHEAT CAKES
BLACK CURRANT CONSERVE   NARBONNE HONEY
OXFORD MARMALADE
WATERCRESS

WHITE STAR LINE

April 14, 1912

2ᴺᴰ CLASS

BREAKFAST

Fruit

Rolled Oats   Boiled Hominy

Fresh Fish

Yarmouth Bloaters (smoked fish)

Grilled Ox Kidneys & Bacon

American Dry Hash au Gratin

Grilled Sausage, Mashed Potatoes

Grilled Ham & Fried Eggs

Fried Potatoes

Vienna & Graham Rolls

Soda Scones

Buckwheat Cakes, Maple Syrup

Conserve   Marmalade

Tea   Coffee

Watercress

WHITE STAR LINE

April 14, 1912

3ᴿᴰ CLASS

BREAKFAST

Oatmeal Porridge & Milk

Smoked Herrings, Jacket Potatoes

Ham & Eggs

Fresh Bread & Butter

Marmalade   Swedish Bread

Tea   Coffee

Were there any famous people on the ship?

Many of the wealthy people aboard the *Titanic* traveled often and knew each other already. Two of the men in first class came from families who'd been rich for several generations. Their last names were widely recognized on both sides of the Atlantic: Guggenheim and Astor.

Benjamin Guggenheim was an American and one of eleven children. His father had built a fortune in mining and **smelting** metals in the United States and South America. Benjamin and his six brothers went into the family business. In 1912, Benjamin spent much of his time living in Paris, France.

He was traveling on the *Titanic* with his staff, including his **valet**, Victor Giglio, and with French singer Léontine Aubart. Guggenheim was one of the passengers who didn't think the ship was badly damaged when it first hit the iceberg. He sent the women in his group, including Aubart

B. GUGGENHEIM

LÉONTINE AUBART

and female staff members, to one of the lifeboats while he remained on board. Like many others, Guggenheim simply didn't believe that the huge ship was in serious trouble.

Crew members claim that when Guggenheim realized the ship was sinking, he and Giglio went back to their cabins and put on their tuxedos. Guggenheim reportedly said, "We're prepared to go down like gentlemen."

After WWI, the Guggenheim family gradually left

the mining business and scattered across the world. Later generations of Guggenheims have used their money to create museums and form organizations to help others. One of Benjamin's daughters, Peggy, collected modern art and opened a gallery in Venice, Italy. Though Peggy died in 1979, the Peggy Guggenheim Collection is world-famous today.

John Jacob Astor IV may have been the richest person on the *Titanic*. He, too, had joined his family business as a young man. The Astors owned large amounts of land in New York City. Astor first helped manage the family properties, then became a real estate developer. He volunteered his own **yacht** and helped supply the US military with weapons during the Spanish-American War in 1898. He was later commissioned as a colonel in the US Volunteers.

JOHN J. ASTOR IV

He and his wife, Madeleine, had just completed a yearlong trip to Europe when they decided to return to the United States on the *Titanic*. They boarded in France with three servants.

Astor was another passenger who thought the collision was a small matter. But when the lifeboats began to launch, he and his group went on deck. Astor was able to put his wife on a boat, but he wasn't allowed to get on with her.

Witnesses said that he finally tried to hold on to the side of one of the last rafts and failed.

Madeleine returned safely to New York, where she gave birth to a son on August 14. She named him John Jacob Astor VI.

Were there animals on the ship?

Like many ships, the *Titanic* probably had a cat on board as a **mascot**. According to one surviving crew member, her name was Jenny, and she and her kittens lived in the **galley** area. Cats on ships could be pets, but they also had a job to do. They helped keep rats and mice away from the food.

Quite a few first- and second-class passengers brought their pets along. Mrs. Ella Holmes White had purchased four French roosters and hens to take home to New York. Another passenger was reported to have a canary.

Most of the animal passengers, though, were dogs. The *Titanic* may have carried a dozen or more breeds. The ship had scheduled a dog show to take place during the voyage. A special crew member was assigned to care for the large dogs below deck.

The dogs housed in the *Titanic's* kennel included Airedales and fox terriers, a champion French bulldog, and a King Charles spaniel.

Some small dogs managed to avoid the kennels because their owners snuck them into their staterooms on higher decks.

In the chaos of the disaster someone freed the kennel dogs, but none escaped the ship. Neither did the birds. Of all the animals on board, only two tiny dogs—a Pomeranian called Lady, and a Pekingese named Sun Yat Sen—survived. Their owners hid them underneath their coats and carried them to the safety of the lifeboats.

How did the *Titanic* sink?

Late in the night on Sunday, April 14, the weather had turned cold. Most passengers had gone to their cabins, and many were already asleep.

In the ship's Marconi Room, wireless engineers Harold Bride and Jack Phillips were sending and receiving telegraph messages. The machine had broken down earlier that day, and there was a backlog waiting. While he was working, Bride took a message from another steamship in Atlantic waters. The SS *Californian* advised him that it was surrounded by chunks of ice. Although earlier messages had warned of icebergs, this was different—and very important—information. But Bride never passed the update to the officers on the **bridge**.

At around the same time, crew member Frederick Fleet was on night watch up in the crow's nest, high above the top deck. His job as lookout was to alert the bridge of anything he saw that might endanger the ship. That night, Fleet and his partner had to rely on their eyesight in the darkness, because

the *Titanic* didn't provide binoculars for lookouts.

Even without binoculars, Fleet saw something shortly before midnight. At first, it only looked like a huge black object. He sent a signal—three bell rings—to the bridge that something was ahead. But as the ship got closer, he used the telephone in the crow's nest to call the bridge.

"Iceberg, right ahead!" he warned them. As the ship began

turning to its port, or left side, Fleet heard a "slight grinding noise." He saw pieces of ice fall on the upper deck. Somewhere beneath the water, the ship's **bow** struck the iceberg. It was 11:40 P.M.

At first, no one believed any serious damage had been

done. Fleet finished his watch and went off duty. Throughout the ship, passengers reacted to the crash, but many were not frightened or upset by the impact.

"It was just as though we went over about a thousand marbles," said one first-class passenger.

"We were awakened by the shock . . . and the stopping of the engines," a passenger in second class reported. A third-class passenger whose cabin was in the front of the ship near the impact had a different report.

"I heard some terrible noise," he said. *"I jumped out on the floor, and the first thing I knew my feet were getting wet."*

What neither Fleet nor the passengers realized was that the *Titanic* had not only hit the 50- or 60-foot iceberg—the ice had damaged the ship's hull. Six of the brand-new watertight compartments flooded so quickly that the ship's pumps couldn't keep up. With all that added water, the ship was too heavy to stay afloat. The wireless operators began sending SOS calls to any nearby ships, including the *Californian* and

the RMS *Carpathia*. The *Titanic* also fired off its distress rockets.

Only an hour after the collision, Captain Smith ordered the crew to lower the lifeboats. Still, many passengers didn't understand how serious the situation was, and there was no panic yet. When the first lifeboat launched at 12:45 A.M., it was not even half full of the sixty-five people it could hold. All those aboard were first-class passengers.

Crew members began to urge passengers to put on their life jackets and get to the top decks. As water filled the lower decks, third-class passengers tried to scramble up. They were delayed at first by locked gates leading to the upper decks, which were later opened.

The captain issued a "women and children first" order for filling the remaining lifeboats, although some women were afraid or unwilling to leave their husbands and adult sons. By 1:45 A.M. at least ten of the sixteen lifeboats were in the water, though there were still hundreds of passengers and crew aboard. Panic began as crew members tried frantically to get the last boats into the water. It was clear that there would not be enough for everyone.

Survivors who did manage to row away could see the bow sinking. They watched in horror and amazement as the **stern** rose up at an angle out of the water, tossing those who remained on the decks into the freezing ocean. The smokestacks broke loose from their cables and crashed down. Then, they heard what sounded like explosions.

The *Titanic* broke in two. First the bow, and then the stern disappeared into the water.

By 2:20 A.M. on April 15, the unthinkable had happened. The great *Titanic* was gone, along with more than 1,500 passengers and crew members. It had taken less than three hours for the "unsinkable" ship to sink.

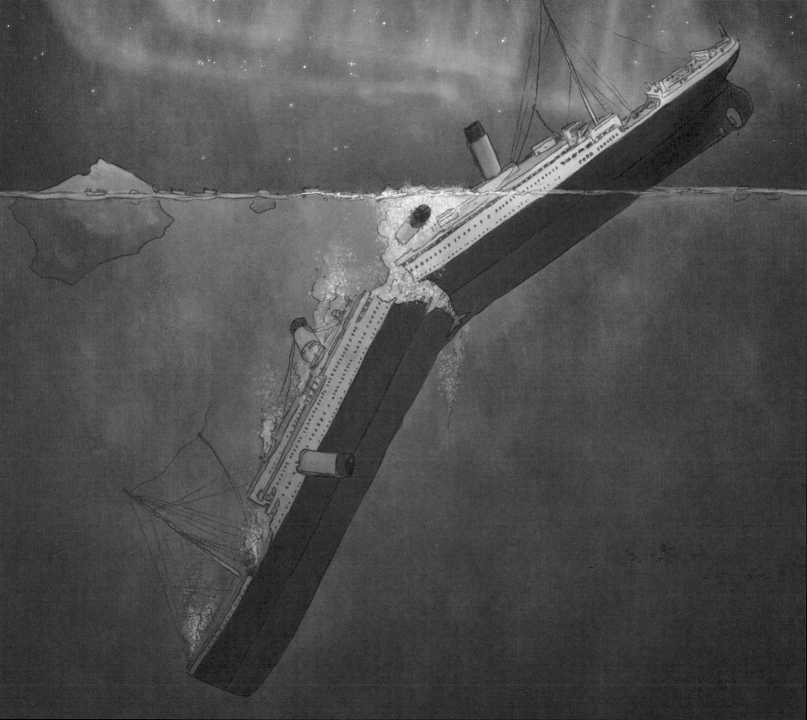

Did the band really keep playing as the ship sank?

Like most luxury ocean liners, the *Titanic* had an orchestra. These musicians played live music during meals and at Sunday religious services on board the ships. During many voyages, an orchestra might also give concerts and play at fancy dances, or balls.

The *Titanic*'s small orchestra was made up of a bandmaster and seven other men who played piano, cello, bass, and violin.

According to many survivors, the orchestra assembled that night and began playing as the *Titanic*'s lifeboats were lowered. Although no one now knows exactly what music they played, it was widely believed that one of their last songs was a hymn called "Nearer My God to Thee."

None of the *Titanic* orchestra survived.

More than four hundred musicians gathered a month later in London at the Royal Albert Hall to play at a concert held to honor those eight men.

Who rescued the survivors?

The *Carpathia*, a Cunard cruise ship, had left New York traveling in the opposite direction of the *Titanic*. It was a much smaller transatlantic ship that had two regular routes: one carried vacationers to the Mediterranean; the other carried immigrants to America. That night, *Carpathia* was about 60 miles away from the site of the *Titanic* disaster.

When Captain Arthur Rostron received word of the trouble, he immediately changed course. He directed his crew to head at full steam for the *Titanic*, knowing that *Carpathia* might be in danger of icebergs as well. In fact, the ship passed six of them along the way.

In the meantime, the rest of the crew prepared to take on as many *Titanic* survivors as they could—despite the fact that the *Carpathia* already carried 700 passengers. Crew members collected extra blankets and prepared warm food and drinks. They located available rooms and set up makeshift hospitals. They set off rockets and Roman candles to help direct the survivors toward their ship.

The first *Titanic* lifeboat was spotted at 4:10 A.M. on April 15. The *Carpathia*'s crew lowered rope ladders, slings,

and even sacks to lift survivors onto the ship's decks. Many survivors had left the *Titanic* wearing only nightclothes. Some women still had on their evening gowns. The *Titanic* survivors were in shock, both from the incident and from the icy cold. Some were injured. Many had suffered the loss of family or friends.

By early morning, *Carpathia*'s passengers were waking up to the incredible scene. They offered what sympathy and help they could. A few even gave up their cabins.

The ship's wireless operators were overloaded with countless requests to send news and messages about what happened. The ship finally set sail for New York at 8:50 A.M., more than four hours after setting out on its brave and risky mission. The *Carpathia* had rescued 712 people.

How many people survived?

The *Carpathia*'s crew members made a list of the survivors on board to send ahead to New York. It was still unclear at that point whether others might have escaped the *Titanic* somehow, or been picked up later by the *Californian* or any other ships. When the *Carpathia* docked in New York on April 18, crowds of anxious people from every walk of life were waiting.

The real truth of the disaster was shocking for everyone. They soon discovered that no other survivors had been found.

Out of 324 first-class passengers, 201 survived.

Out of 284 second-class passengers, 118 survived.

Out of 709 third-class passengers, only 181 survived.

Only 212 of the almost 891 men and women of the crew survived.

But there were joyful reunions for some. Two French toddlers were put into the last lifeboat by their father, who did not survive. The boys couldn't speak English, so a passenger who spoke French took care of them in New York while officials tried to locate their mother. A few days later, a picture of them appeared in a French newspaper and their mother recognized them. Kind strangers raised the money to bring her to New York, where she was reunited with Michel and Edmond Navratil.

The youngest person to survive the *Titanic* was two-month-old Millvina Dean. Her mother and brother, Bertram, also survived. Millvina grew up to become the last remaining survivor of the disaster. She lived to be 97 years old. She was a celebrity when she died in England in May 2009.

How was news of the *Titanic* spread around the world?

The first news of the disaster was sent in a wireless message by Captain Rostron after the *Titanic* passengers came aboard the *Carpathia*. Newspapers, hungry for details, tried sending messages to the ship. The captain ordered that only outgoing messages be sent, so that survivors could send news to their families.

Rostron didn't know that *Carpathia* passenger Carlos Hurd, a journalist, was already interviewing survivors. Hurd worked for the *St. Louis Post-Dispatch* newspaper. He knew he couldn't send his exclusive story to the paper without someone noticing. So he sent a wireless message to a friend in New York who was a reporter, too. His paper, the *New York Evening World*, sent a tugboat that pulled alongside the *Carpathia* as it came into New York Harbor.

Other reporters had similar ideas. They crowded onto tugs, yelling up questions to the *Carpathia* through megaphones.

The captain threatened to shoot both the determined reporters and anyone who helped them.

Hurd wrote his story, sealed it, and secretly tossed it overboard to the *New York Evening World* reporters waiting on the tug. His story was straight from the mouths of the *Titanic* survivors. It hit the newsstands in the evening edition of the *New York Evening World*—the same day the *Carpathia* docked.

Did anything change after the *Titanic* sank?

The sinking of the *Titanic* shocked the shipping industry worldwide. When the *Carpathia* docked in New York, two US senators met Ismay at his cabin before he could even leave the ship.

They announced that they were holding an inquiry into the cause of the disaster that very next day at the Waldorf Astoria hotel, which had been built by John Jacob Astor IV. The senators wanted Ismay and other passengers and crew to testify under oath about the details of the *Titanic*'s final hours.

Ismay had seemed especially disturbed after his rescue, staying isolated in his cabin on the *Carpathia*. Other survivors found it suspicious that

the president of the White Star Line had entered a lifeboat in the first place. They also resented the fact that on the *Carpathia* he didn't try to console or visit with them. Many newspapers even suggested he was a coward for being alive.

Hearings were held in both New York City and Washington, DC. Ismay was one of several dozen survivors who testified in person or in writing by **affidavit**. A separate British inquiry began weeks later.

The final US report was issued May 28, 1912. The inquiry found that what happened to the *Titanic* was indeed an accident, but it was an accident that should never have claimed so many lives. The British report was issued on July 30. It came to almost the same conclusion.

Both reports recommended these major changes in **maritime** law, creating new rules for all ships in the industry:

1. There should be 24-hour wireless communication and the necessary number of crew members to operate it.
2. There must be enough lifeboats for all passengers and crew. The *Titanic* had only enough lifeboats

for 1,178 passengers, when there were more than 2,200 passengers on board. More lifeboats could have saved hundreds more lives.

3. A skilled crew should be assigned to each lifeboat before a voyage and the crew should have regular lifeboat drills.
4. Every ship should be equipped with searchlights.
5. Design and construction of ships should be improved to include stronger watertight compartments.

These new rules would make ships safer, but they still had to navigate the ice fields of the North Atlantic. In 1914, an international group of shipping companies met to create a permanent ice patrol, led by the US Coast Guard.

Today the International Ice Patrol is still on its mission. From February 1 through July 31, during ice season, the US Coast Guard uses aircraft and radar to check ice conditions in the area near the Grand Banks of Newfoundland. The Canadian Ice Service takes over the work in the "off-season" and partners with the United States in emergencies.

What happened to *Titanic*'s "sister" ships?

Though the *Titanic* met a tragic end, *Olympic* continued to sail until 1935. *Britannic*, the "youngest sister," had its keel laid in November 1911, but new safety rules after the *Titanic* disaster caused its design to change a great deal. The ship was still being fitted out when WWI broke out in Europe in 1914. It was called into service with the British Navy as a hospital ship in 1915. *Britannic* made six military voyages in the Mediterranean Sea, but struck a **mine** and sank on November 21, 1916.

Harland and Wolff remained in the sailing industry, becoming a leader in shipbuilding and engineering well into the twenty-first century.

The White Star Line was sold in 1927. A few years later, both the Cunard and White Star lines were in financial trouble. In 1934, the former rivals merged to form the

Cunard White Star Limited. By 1949, the company had dropped the White Star name.

Today Cunard is still one of the most well-known international cruise ship companies.

Was the *Titanic* wreckage ever found?

Attempts to find the *Titanic* began almost immediately in the days after the disaster. White Star Line hired extra ships to search the ocean area near Halifax, Nova Scotia, in Canada. The remains of 328 passengers were recovered and other debris from the *Titanic* was found. The exact location of the *Titanic* was not discovered for another seventy-three years.

American Robert Ballard, a marine scientist and oceanographer for the US Navy, had been interested in shipwrecks since he was a boy. In addition to doing underwater research, in the 1970s he helped develop a three-person **submersible** with a mechanical arm. In 1977, he tried using his knowledge to find the *Titanic* wreck. His attempt failed.

In 1985, Ballard got a second chance.

He'd designed *Argo*, a new submersible sled with a remote-controlled camera. The US Navy asked Ballard to use *Argo* to find out what happened to two submarines that had sunk in the North Atlantic. In exchange, the navy gave him permission to also search for the resting place of the *Titanic*.

Ballard's team worked with a French research team from the French Institute for the Exploitation of the Sea. During their search for the submarines, Ballard discovered that ocean

currents affect the way debris sinks. He returned to the same area he'd searched before. This time, he found that the *Titanic* had left a trail of debris as it broke apart and sank to the ocean floor.

On September 1, 1985, *Argo*'s cameras sent pictures of the ship's boilers—13,000 feet below the surface. Soon afterward, *Argo* sent more video. The *Titanic*'s bow and stern rested in two pieces on the ocean floor. The hull appeared to be upright. No one had ever really forgotten the *Titanic*, but Robert Ballard's discovery that day sparked new public interest in the ship. It also opened the door to other scientists, who began to study the wreckage. They hoped to use more new technology to find out not only what happened to the *Titanic*, but how the great ship went down.

Was there any treasure on the ship?

No treasure chest of gold has ever been found in the *Titanic* wreckage. However, a leather pouch filled with expensive diamond, ruby, and gold jewelry was recovered!

In the early days and weeks after the disaster, many items were found floating in the ocean off the Grand Banks of Newfoundland and off the coast of Nova Scotia. Life jackets, dinner plates, sections of carpet, a chair, and a violin were found in the debris. Amazingly, even some letters and

postcards survived in the water. Many of the personal items were returned to the families.

Decades later, people still hoped to find pieces of *Titanic* history. If any treasure *was* found, who might it belong to? The courts had to decide.

A US **salvage** company called RMS *Titanic* Inc. won legal rights in 1994 to be the only company allowed to collect artifacts from the site. The salvagers promised not to sell what they found, but to "preserve history." Their biggest find was the pouch of jewelry, which became part of a 100th Anniversary *Titanic* exhibit in 2012.

Thousands of *Titanic* artifacts exist today. Some were collected by scientists or salvagers, and others kept as souvenirs by survivors or their families. Many are on display at *Titanic* museums around the world. And still more remain undisturbed in the deep, on the ocean floor.

Can people visit the wreckage?

Scientist and salvagers haven't been the only people filled with curiosity about seeing the *Titanic* over the years. Since the ship was located, tourist expeditions have become big business for those rich enough to afford the trip.

The first non-scientist tourists visited the site in 1998 as part of a dive organized by a private company. The twelve men and women on the tour took a Russian submersible vessel 2.5 miles down to see the wreckage and the debris field. A judge had issued a court order against the trip, since rights had already been given to RMS *Titanic* Inc.

However, the tourist expedition business continued to grow. Today, a *Titanic* expedition might include much more than a simple submersible trip. Different companies offer special experiences. Some take visitors on a multi-hour "tour" of the *Titanic* wreckage and the huge debris field surrounding it. Other companies give tourists a crash course in using science equipment, so they can experience working alongside researchers to map and take pictures of the site. The cost of these vacations starts at around $150,000!

Are the *Titanic* movies true?

The story of the *Titanic*, its passengers, crew, and tragic end has fascinated the public since they saw the first newspaper headlines in April 1912. Its sinking was an international disaster that has been portrayed in documentaries and countless movies. But from the very beginning, what moviegoers saw on the big screen was sometimes a mix of fact and fiction—and often, much more fiction than fact!

Surprisingly, the very first *Titanic* movie was released May 16, 1912—only a month after the ship went down. *Saved from the* Titanic was a silent film starring an actress who was actually a *Titanic* survivor. Though she made up the characters and storyline, Dorothy Gibson wore the exact same evening dress, sweater, and shoes she had on when she was rescued by the *Carpathia*. The film was shot on location in New Jersey and on an abandoned cargo ship in New York Harbor. *Saved from the* Titanic was a hit. No one had seen anything like it. But the stress of reliving the experience may

have been too much for Dorothy Gibson. She quit the movie business after making the film. No copies of it exist today.

The British film *A Night to Remember* (1958) was based on a famous nonfiction book about the *Titanic*. American writer Walter Lord's research included interviews with sixty-four living *Titanic* survivors. Lord's 1955 book was the most carefully researched one to date about the wreck. It became a bestseller. When producer William MacQuitty heard about the book, he quickly bought the film rights. As a young boy, he had watched the *Titanic* leave Belfast as it set sail to Southampton after its construction was completed. The actors in *A Night to Remember* portrayed many of the real passengers and crew members. Like Walter Lord's book, the film stuck closely to known facts and actual experiences.

One movie that is often mentioned in connection with the *Titanic* is called *The Unsinkable Molly Brown*. This musical was released in 1964. The film is less about the *Titanic* and more about the life of one of its survivors, first-class passenger Margaret Tobin Brown.

She was a rich, independent woman from Colorado. After evacuating the *Titanic*, she is said to have helped row her lifeboat. Some reports also say she attempted to get the men in the boat to turn around to

MARGARET BROWN

save anyone who might be in the water. They refused. Once on the *Carpathia*, Brown organized its wealthy passengers and collected nearly $10,000 to help other survivors who had lost everything.

The facts about Margaret's life before the *Titanic* were close to the truth, but the biggest fiction was her nickname. A writer actually came up with "The Unsinkable Molly Brown" name after the disaster. Margaret was never called "Molly" by people who knew her in her lifetime.

Of course, James Cameron's *Titanic* (1997) introduced the story to a new generation. His all-star cast of actors and incredible special effects brought the disaster to life in a way no other film had, or could. This *Titanic* focused on fictional main characters. It re-created much of the original interior of the ship and captured the drama of the *Titanic*'s final moments. Cameron visited the wreckage site himself in preparing for the film, and he asked *A Night to Remember* author Walter Lord to consult on the film. It is one of the highest-grossing movies of all time.

Will the *Titanic* ever be raised from the ocean?

It is extremely unlikely that the *Titanic* will ever see daylight again. It has become home to sea life such as coral, crabs, sea anemones, and many varieties of fish. What's left of the ship

is not only too fragile for such a move, but it is being eaten alive.

A 2019 deep exploration team spent a week examining the wreckage. This was the first time in several years that new pictures and video were taken. The images showed that parts of the ship that were clearly visible two decades ago have now disintegrated and in some cases disappeared. The reason for this, according to Halifax scientist Henrietta Mann, is that a species of bacteria is eating the ship's iron. The iron breaks down into drip-like shapes that she calls "rustcicles."

Even without the bacteria, sea currents and sea water would naturally cause the ship to deteriorate over time. Increased activity from tourist expeditions may be speeding up the process. Now scientists around the world want to try to slow it down.

The first big step in attempting to protect the site came in 2012 when the wreckage was named a UNESCO cultural heritage site. UNESCO (the United Nations Educational, Scientific and Cultural Organization) encourages countries to cooperate with each other in saving historical museums and monuments.

And in January 2020 the United States announced it had signed an international treaty with Britain in which the two countries agreed to protect and preserve the *Titanic* site. The countries have invited Canada and France to sign on, as well. They will work together to issue permits for visiting or removing artifacts. Their hope is that together, they can limit the traffic around the wreckage.

How much longer will the *Titanic* wreckage last? No one knows. It is a special place that many people believe deserves to be respected. Whatever the future holds for the "unsinkable" *Titanic*, the tragic story of its passengers and crew will certainly remain unforgettable.

Glossary

Affidavit: a written statement confirmed by oath

Bow: the forward, or front, part of a ship

Bridge: the place where the controls are on a ship

Galley: a ship's kitchen

Hulls: the frames or bodies of ships

Immigrate: to come to another country to live

Keel: the ridge or blade on the bottom of a ship, on which the hull is built

Luxury: something that is very fancy, pleasant, or rich

Maritime: related to the sea

Mascot: an animal or object chosen as a good luck symbol

Merged: two or more items joined together to form one

Mine: an explosive hidden underground or underwater

Promenade: a public place for walking or strolling

Salvage: something useful or valuable that is recovered or saved

Smelting: the process of melting rock that contains a metal, in order to separate out the metal

Stern: the rear end of a boat or ship

Submersible: an underwater vehicle

Transatlantic: crossing the Atlantic Ocean

Valet: a male servant

Yacht: a large sailboat, often used for cruises or racing